SMOKES AND WHISKEY

TEJASWINI DIVYA NAIK

This is a work of Poetry. Names, characters, businesses, places, events and incidents are either product's of the author's imagination or used in a fictitious manner. Any resemblance to actual persons, living or dead, or actual events is purely coincidental.

First Print : January 2018
Seventh Print: August 2022
Printed in India

Printed at Parksons Graphics Pvt. Ltd.
Typeset in Palatino Linotype

ISBN: 978-93-87269-40-8
Cover design: Tejaswini Divya Naik

STORYMIRROR
Stories that reflect you

Publisher: StoryMirror Infotech Pvt. Ltd.
7th Floor, El Tara Building, Behind Delphi Building,
Hiranandani Gardens, Powai - 400076, Mumbai, India.

Web: storymirror.com
Facebook: @storymirror
Twitter: @story_mirror
Instagram: @storymirror
Email: marketing@storymirror.com

Statutory Warning: *The poet, her models, the publisher, and anyone associated with this book, DO NOT promote and/or encourage Drinking and Smoking. Drinking and Smoking is injurious to health.*

"Smokes & Whiskey is a stellar compilation of sing-songesque, lyrical poems. Penned with pizzazz by Tejaswini Naik, the poems beautifully capture the journeys of a lost heart and a battered soul.
With her fresh style, Tejaswini has managed to strike an envious balance between contemporary styles of writing and a pictorial representation of an artist's emotions.
She truly is a master poetess."
- Sanyukta Iyer, Senior Correspondent, Mumbai Mirror - A Times of India publication.

"In *Smokes and Whiskey*, poet-extraordinaire Tejaswini Divya Naik sets out to find hope in the most unlikely of places: in the raw and sometimes brutal reality of our lives. This book of poems is as refreshing as it is important. In an original voice, Naik refuses the romantic idealism over-wrought clichés so often found in today's social media poetry. Instead, she dives head first into such topics as domestic abuse and lost love. But she does so with the care and tenderness of a powerful poetess."
- Nate Proctor, Author, Speaker, Story-teller, Art Curator and Social Media Influencer

"I have known Tejaswini since she was in college and her love of literature was as intense then as it is now. I always knew one day she would write a beautiful book of her own. 'Smokes and Whiskey' is that book - exquisitely laid out and lovingly worded. I look forward to many more books in the years ahead."
- Devapriya Roy, Author (The Vague Women's Handbook, The Weight Loss Club, The Heat and Dust Project)

"One who leads by example, who shares with her heart, someone who inspires and encourages other women, whose energy is contagious, that's (what/who) you are to me, Tej. I can't remember a writer having such an impact on me. I've always been inspired by your writing. It's like I've found a voice to put my story out there. Every word, every poem feels so personal and that really is something that can resonate with a lot of people. I'm sure this book will inspire a lot of readers.

Thank you for encouraging me to draw and for giving me the opportunity to be a part of SatinandGold and then, Smokes and Whiskey.

Will forever be grateful for your support!

Here's to many more!"

Love,

Husnul, Illustrator

"Precise articulation with perfect metaphors which instil a bittersweet pain inside your heart, stirring emotions you didn't notice you had. Tejaswini Divya Naik has always possessed the power to make people 'feel'. And that is just what she does in her first ever book of poetries; a beautiful, riveting compilation of the intensely exhilarating, liberating yet binding, soul-crushing emotions we've all been through - Love, Heartbreak, and Healing."

- *Ambuja Naik. (Empath, Psychologist, Actor, and also the proud younger sister of the poetess.)*

"Touching each emotional chord, Smokes & Whiskey is sure to take you on a roller coaster of sentiments with the literary prose, well balanced photography and contemporary poetry. Keep up with the creative depths in writing with this one despite it being a debut!"

- *Sristi Sinha, Social Media Strategist & Food Blogger (The Food Sinner)*

"When you read T's poems, you're hit by a sense of tragedy and trauma, and somehow when all of this tragedy unravels itself- you witness a bout of callous happiness that seems so fulfilling, so wholesome.
I am honored to be a part of this, I hope Smokes & Whiskey goes on to become a force to reckon with, and so does she."
- Srishti Bose, Corporate Lawyer/Model

"This book has been one of the best visual and poetic journeys I've ever experienced. The writer is immensely skilled and triggers all your hidden emotions. She makes you travel through her poetry in a compelling way, making you feel exactly what was intended. A must read for everyone who's ever experienced this strange feeling called love, and the repercussions of its failure!"
- Yash Bhardwaj, CEO & Founder - Indian Memes

"A heart touching book that gives you the strength you need to carry on. Wonderfully written, and definitely a book I'd read in order to gain solace."
- Virali Modi, BBC 100 Women, Rising Star India '17, Youth Ambassador - Enable Travel, Disability Rights Activist, Founder of #MyTrainToo and #RampMyRestaurant

"satinandgold – Tejaswini's username pretty much describes everything that her Instagram is about. Her writings are bold and beautiful just like she is. She has the unique quality of lending a personal and relatable perspective to her pieces that sure melt the heart. This book in your hands is an extravagant piece of work you'll sure fall in love with!"
- Tuheena Raj, Corporate Finance Professional at Citibank India; Writer (@wordsofworth)

"Before you get into this book, readers, let me ask you - have you ever heard of the calm before the storm? Of course, you have. Now close your eyes and imagine that, but now, I want you to compare the calm with the ocean of emotions you've kept bottled up inside. As you think about it more, can you feel the tides drifting and rising slowly but surely? Can you feel the storm gathering? Do you see the storm approaching you timidly, but all at once? Good, that means you'll now be prepared for the beautiful storm these absolutely soul crushing and completely heart wrenching poems will raise within you. Have fun sailing, ladies and gents. And to Tejaswini, I am beyond proud of each of your accomplishments and I cannot wait for all your plans to take me by surprise.

Being there from the start and know how of this book to helping you edit a few of these wonderful poems has been nothing short of a pleasure and I cannot wait for the world to be amazed by you."

- *Anusha Mishra, Copywriter & Social Media Manager*

Thank you, dear love, for scorching me.
Thank you, dear wildfire, for engulfing me.
Thank you, dear smoke, for mellowing me.
Thank you, dear ashes, for letting me crumble.
Thank you for everything.
For if not,
The wings of this Phoenix wouldn't have flown.

Graphics by Husnul "Oon" Shaikh

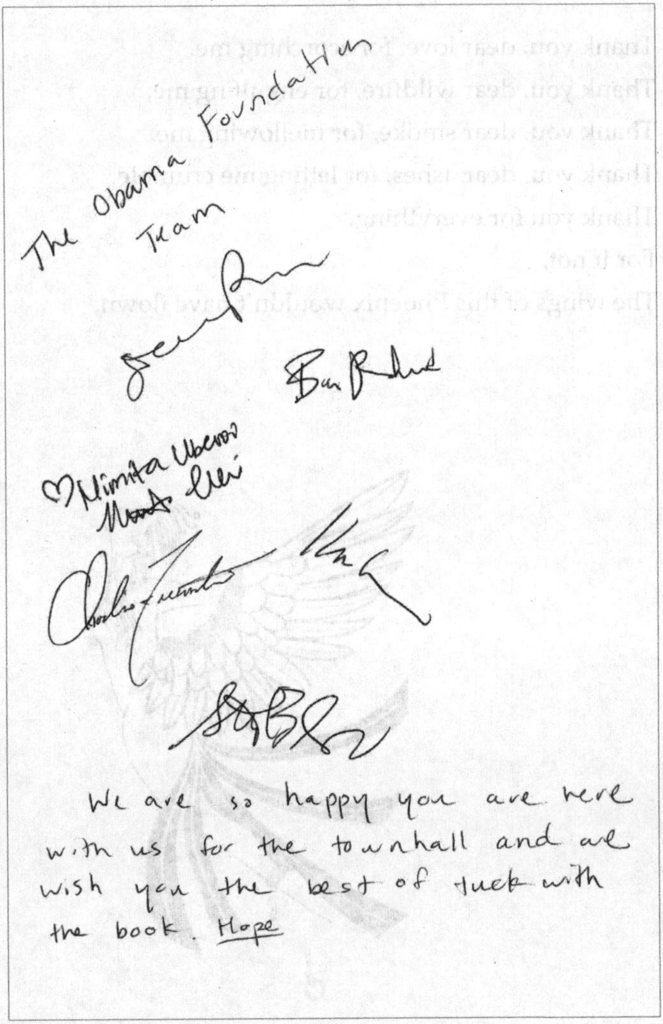
The Obama Foundation Team

We are so happy you are here with us for the townhall and we wish you the best of luck with the book. Hope

Recognition from The Obama Foundation

FOREWORD

This book is an act of courage.

To love is a very brave thing to do. Even when it is one of those things that is so common every day and everyone you know is living it. However, offering one's expressions and experiences bare to the world, transcends into a higher level of love and courage. And that is exactly what the next few pages will reveal to you.

Every escapade with love is unique. No story can entirely be the same. No series of highs and lows, either. And yet, Smokes and Whiskey unravels in a run-of-the-mill but unique journey. It's a bold take on moving ahead, while simultaneously confronting your past and realizing your present. This journey will certainly leave you breathless.

This book will take you through the highs of it but then will really take you to the lows of being in love, especially being in love as a woman. Woven into this tapestry of poetry are the aggressive colours of violence and pain, not uncommon for many, especially women.

One of my favorite pieces of work in this anthology of poems is 'I give hearts out away for free'. Tejaswini delivers a poem that captures the essence and beauty of language through her words, while several other works draw extensively from her personal triumphs and tribulations. They also drive home the point that, "to love is the essence of life". And yet, sometimes, maybe a lot of times, love is the most painful thing.

I hope, as it did for me, it tears you apart and stitches you back again.

Like love does.

Like life does.

But in this case, with some smoke and whiskey.

Preethi Herman

(Preethi is a friend of the poet/author and heads Change.org India)

Wishes from Barkha Dutt

THE BEGINNING

There can be no greater pride for parents than to see their chubby cheek and dimpled chin bundle of joy metamorphose from a happy – go – lucky child to an intellectually profound and mature thought leader.

Tejaswini, our daughter, has been blessed with an insatiable literary appetite and had a natural preference for books which have stood the test of time.

She has been a staunch and persuasive champion of social justice and taken up the cause of equality for women and stood up against any oppression and suppression of basic civil liberties and rights.

Her first book, with a title of **"Smokes and Whiskey"** seemed a bit rebellious for teetotaler parents like us who also do not smoke, and though we have been her strongest critics, we are also her strongest supporters.

The poems manage to be vivid and thought provoking, without being morbid or negative; and definitely are far away from being vulgar.

They reflect the "angst" of acceptance and rejection, warm welcomes and farewells, and through it all shines a fortitude of spirit and hope and forgiveness to negotiate the twists and turns of complex interactions.

We, as parents, wish her the best in this journey of discovery and revelations.

We hope you enjoy reading it as much as we did!

- Col. (Dr.) Anurag Naik and Divya Naik

Vijay Rupani

Chief Minister, Gujarat State

apro/Jm/2018/02/15/dt

Dt. 15/02/2018

Chi. Tejaswini,

Saprem Ashirvad.

I am in receipt of your letter and a copy of the anthology of your poems. Thank you.

Even though the Title **"Smokes and Whiskey"** misleads the common reader to anticipate the outburst of youthful revolt against the conservative societal norms, the subtle emotions emanating from the tender words of all the poems throw light on the intricate sentiments of a woman. The element of love is a universal phenomenon, though its effects may differ from person to person. Your anthology stands alone, among many outbursts of emotional writings, just because it has a fragrance of truthfulness towards the internal being of womanhood.

I extend my heartiest best wishes to you and your Anthology for the grand success among the people who love, adore and worship the might of pen and creativity. I also extend my sincere respects to your parents who have let you grow like a wild but independent flower and blossom at will.

(Vijay Rupani)

Graphics by Husnul "Oon" Shaikh

ACKNOWLEDGEMENTS

"What's coming will come and we'll face it when it does".
Hagrid, from The Goblet of Fire.

And so, here we are. Facing it, head on, calm and composed, without fear, without the plausibility of being judged, all bags and baggage dropped. But without a few people in my life, this boat wouldn't have sailed off so here goes…

First and foremost, a huge thank you to my parents, Col. (Dr.) Anurag Naik and Divya Naik. If not for their constant support and trust in me, I wouldn't have taken the first step towards publishing this book. To me, their words are carved in stone. Because of them, I've learnt most of life's intriguing lessons.

I would like to thank (and hug – *just because she's not a hugger*) my sister, because she's my critique first and then my best friend . You are my rock.

My friends have been my constant. Thank you, Sristi, for tolerating my dramas and tantrums. Thank you being the best friend I can constantly disturb.
Thank you, Anusha, for the proofreading sessions, and being the silent editor I never knew I needed.

You were my first fan, Husnul, and I could never imagine this book without you. Thank you for illustrating my first book. Thank you, Sanyukta, for being the lifeline I never knew I had. For always being more excited and pumped up about my writing than I could ever be.

A heartfelt shout out to Srishti, Nida, Ambika and Ambuja; my beautiful models.

Thank you, Pooja and Riza, and the exemplary photographers who allowed me ever so lovingly to use their pictures. Amar, without you I wouldn't have met Anirudh and Amneet and without these two, this book would never have reached StoryMirror, without whom this entire boat would've drowned. So thank you, for accepting me and my book and letting me realize that publishing my work and my voice matters. Super special mention to this gem - Ankit, for always pushing and prodding me on, no matter how exhausted I am.

I'd like to thank Muffin, a human par excellence running around in a dog avatar, for patiently sitting through and listening to my cries of anguish and anger. Thank you, Muffin, for licking all my troubles far far away.

I'd like to end with a quote by my favourite author, J. K. Rowling – my inspiration.

"Phoenixes burst into flame when it is time for them to die and are reborn from the ashes".

Thank you, Ms Rowling, now watch me fly.

Tejaswini Divya Naik

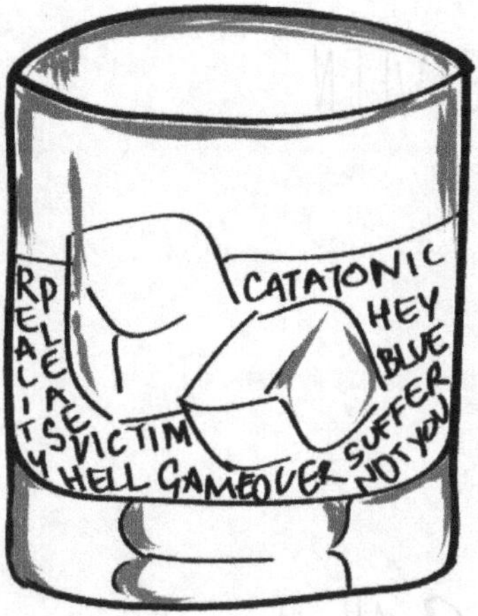

index

PART 1: THE FALL

1 Hey

2 Eternity

3 The Lion

Graphics by Husnul "Oon" Shaikh

PART 2: THE IN BETWEEN

4 Good

5 A Hidden Rainbow

6 In Love

7 Of Satin & Gold & All Things Bold

Graphics by Husnul "Oon" Shaikh

PART 3: THE DOWNFALL

8 Smile

9 Train Wreck

10 Infinity

11 Furthermore

12 Thorn Rose

13 Invisible Ink

14 View

15 Inconclusive

16 Nothing

17 Resuscitate

18 Obsolete

Graphics by Husnul "Oon" Shaikh

19 Lights Out

20 Poison

21 Me

22 Bipolar

23 I C A N ' T B R E A T H E

24 Reality

25 Catatonic

26 Hell

27 Fit

28 Habits

29 Tell Me?

30 Nor You

31 Antagonist

32 Climax

33 Book Of Tragedies

34 Fall Apart

35 Home, Please?

36 Smokes and Whiskey

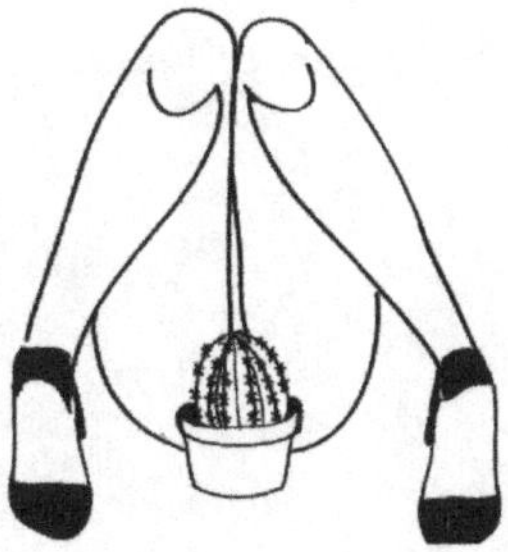

PART 4: THE THEREAFTER

37 Victim

38 Blue

39 Suffer

40 Buh — Bye

41 Game Over

42 Smokes and Whiskey, 2.0

Graphics by Husnul "Oon" Shaikh

JUGNI;

PART 1 : THE FALL

Graphics by Husnul "Oon" Shaikh

Photograph of Srishti Bose by Ashutosh

1.

Kiss me, she said
Make me feel alive again,

Let's dance in the rain
And feel it on our face.

Feel me, she said
I need your lips to call out my name.

Breathe me in,
Like I'm the one running through your veins.

Touch me, she said
Hold me tight
Never let me out of your sight.

Run your fingers through my hair
Caress your lips along the breadth of my skin
Naked and bare.

Heal me,
All the broken parts
And all the hurting
Bring it together,
I'll be your kintsugi.

See me rise
See me fly
I'll be the wings,
You be my sky.

But
Once, at least?
Look at me
Know I exist?
Don't see through me.
See me.
Look at me.
I am here.

Hey.
See me.
Please see me
Once?
Just see me.

Hey.

2.

I give hearts out away for free
Maybe there's something wrong in me

Or maybe it's just a manufacturing default,
as I keep saying over and over again
But to whom and why,
tell me why do I need to explain.

This is me
This is my life
I've got to live it the way I want
And I will live it the way I like
You, with your opinions and suggestions
And you, with your delusional miscalculations
Please.
It's a sincere request
Back the hell off
Leave me be
Let me keep giving my hearts out away for free
Trust me, I'm happy.

Or maybe I am not.
But neither of this is your concern

Photograph of Nida by Riza Suraiya Khan

Please go find another neighbor's house for your
calories to burn.

I give hearts out away for free
And I'll keep at it until eternity.

I am an open book, unopened, yet to read
I give love with zero expectations
My love isn't a binding contract, there ain't no
policies.

So, if and when I get my heart broken or my soul
crushed
And trust another, while I'd sworn to never trust
Or I find solace in some man's hug,
I am not giving you permission to blame
Or to call me names,
This is my life, not your name calling game.

So I'll keep giving hearts out away for free,
Without expecting anything back in return
And I'll keep giving hearts out away for free,
From now, until

Eternity.

Photograph of Srishti Bose by Tanvi Chaudhary

3.

You.

You with your hair falling in your eyes,
Wind blowing in your face,
That hidden somewhere
Deep under the beard smile.

I guess it was that gorgeous
Spring morning,
Sitting at work,
Quietly,
When I saw you
For the first time,

And from then on,
That's all that I saw,
There was no turning back.

Everything changed
But everything was still the same.

From lunches to dinners to protein bars,
From room numbers to counting stars,
From milk and bournvita to vodka and whiskey,
From never taking a risk to everything risky,
From singing songs to singing ad jingles,
From kissing passionately to your devilish tickles,
From my awkward weird self to your beautiful mind,
From your hellos and goodbyes,
To your 'mornings and goodnights.

And the lamb fell in love with,

The Lion.

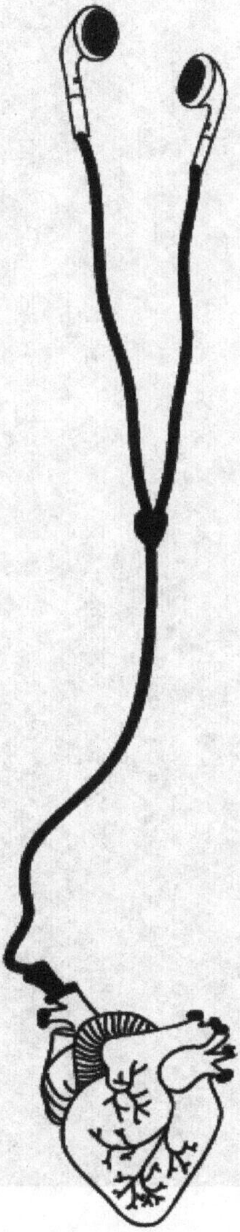

PART 2 : THE IN BETWEEN

Graphics by Husnul "Oon" Shaikh

Photograph of Nida by Riza Suraiya Khan

4.

You've spoilt her
For her own good.

Hidden beneath
Sheaths
And layers,
The girl that no one saw.

She was unknown to the world,
But you made her feel like diamonds and pearls.

The girl that no one knows -
She is black and white vs coloured.

But when it comes to you,
She is
Uncovered,
Naked,
And juxtaposed

Under the stars
And the moon.

Exposed to your ferocious and gentle touch,
Raw as your own body,
She's attuned to your voice and your soul.

She's bound and free,
Calm yet a little more than crazy.

You've
Spoilt
Her
For
Her
Own

Good.

5.

And then he said he loved me.
He said he meant it.
But that he didn't know what love was, or how it felt.
That maybe all he did was just care so deeply,
And care with all he had.

But he was scarred.
And he was scared.
That it was so confusing.
So confusing.

He wanted to hold me,
Look me in the eyes,
Touch
And caress,
Kiss me even.
Hold me till dawn
Brought its' chirping birds on us,
Wake up next to me
Watch the first ray of the sun hitting my face,
And how it illuminated the person
He so deeply cared about.

Photograph of Srishti Bose by Pooja Pandey

But he couldn't understand what this was.
What we had.
His past had screwed him up.
And his past
Was screwing up my right now.
He said he wanted me in his life,
But didn't want to be in a relationship (?)

What were we then?
I asked.
I don't know.
He said.

And all I could do was
Smile.
But all I wanted to do was
Cry,
And have him wipe my tears.
All I wanted was
To lie down on the ground,
Breaking down into
A hundred and one sobs.
But have him be there for me,
And hold me,
And tell me
It was all going to be okay.
But, he wasn't.

So I opened my eyes
And faced the morning.
My eyes seemed to reflect the sombre mood
The weather wore.
The sun being dimmed by an array of clouds,
Pouring down in bucketful and scores

But then, in the midst of it all,
A little far away,

Was an almost visible rainbow,
And maybe that's all the hope I needed to move on.

And maybe that's all that I had in store at that moment.

A Hidden Rainbow.

6.

And in that moment,
They lived a lifetime.

An era of forever,
And then some more.
Their life wasn't any different,
Yet nothing ordinary.

Swooning
And dancing
And laughing
And loving
Fighting
And distancing
And chastising
And patronizing

They were so in love,
That it never felt enough
And the burning
And yearning
And hurting
And healing

Graphics by Husnul "Oon" Shaikh

It all felt so much,
But in the same breath,
So little.

Ten years past
And ten years forward,
They are the same
Two sane beings,
Insane
And in love and in love and

In Love.

Photograph of Tejaswini Divya Naik

7.

For all I am is but,
A mystery.

Forever unknown
Forever hidden.

I want to be
Discovered
To be
Uncovered.

Mask
By
Mask,
Sheath
By
Sheath.

Yet
A layer,
Unfathomable.

Forever procrastinating,
Hardwood and Maple

Silent, yet affable,
Unspoken stories

Yet to unfold

Of Satin & Gold & All Things Bold.

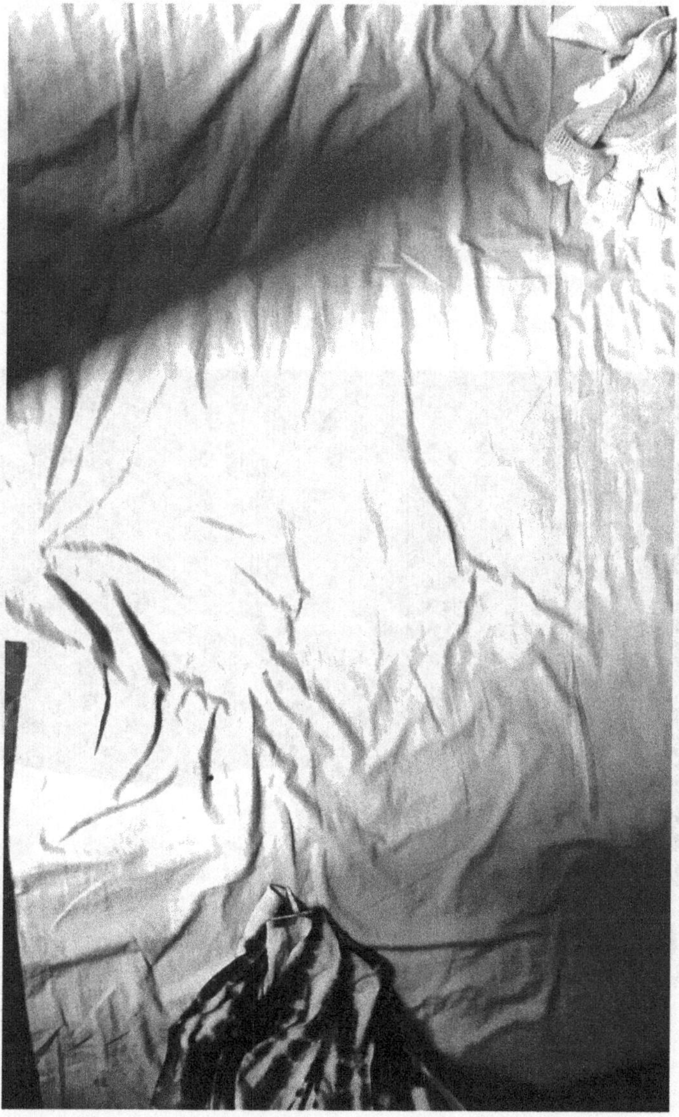

PART 3 : THE DOWNFALL

Photograph by Tejaswini Naik

Photograph of Ambuja Naik by Tejaswini Naik

8.

Brimming with tears,
I am so full
Not too far away,
The same old, same old,
You too are sailing through.

Passengers of the same boat,
Passing through tidal waves
Dangling, I hold onto you,
You leave your support and give me your hands
Making me forever grateful and in awe.

Strong enough to love you,
Weak enough to get hurt on loop.
You and I, we are two sides of the same cassette
Playing and pausing, rewinding, forwarding.
But me, I'm stuck on repeat, on a thread,
dangling.

You say words and more words,
In hopes of pushing me away.
Not realizing,
Those same words are what keeps getting me
closer.
For what no one ever could
You've climbed the walls and broken the mould.

Trying to put up a fight,
I put up my strongest face on
One swish and flick, couple of sentences strewn together,
And there goes the resolve down the drain.
I am done, wide awake and confused,
Stupid, naked and bruised.

This little girl grew up too fast,
Seen too much too soon.
But so have you.
This strong urge is there to just keep holding on,
And like you've been there for me,
I want to be there for you too.

You're music to my ears and comfort to my soul,
Don't think otherwise, you're far away from hurting me
Others exist for that, that's not your job profile,
Because, you're the sole reason

For
Me
To

Smile.

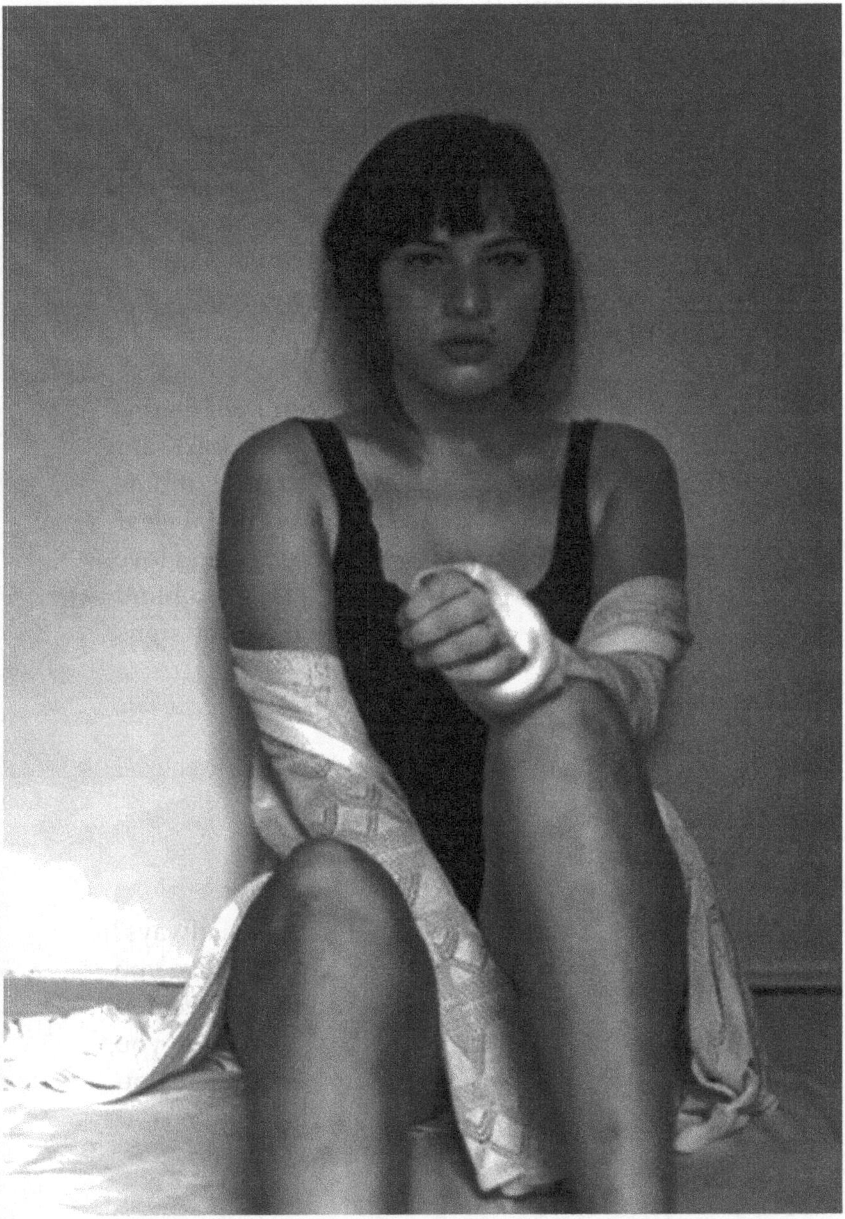

Photograph of Srishti Bose by Pooja Pandey

9.

He messed up,
You got played

Don't tell no one
That's what he'd said.
Since the beginning of time,
It was crystal clear.
But you were in love,
And blind,
Overlooked the signs.

Maybe,
Just maybe,
You deserved this
To be fake loved
And be dissed.

Isn't that what happens, always?
They say they love you
And then leave you,
Abandon you,
Further damage you.

But maybe,
Just maybe,
Since you were a damned fool in love,
You deserved this,
You did.

To be
Hurt
And to be

Left,
Scorched,
Drained,
Blemished,
Derailed.

So
You became
A

Train Wreck.

Photograph of Nida by Riza Suraiya Khan

10.

Damned I'll be
Forever procrastinating
Hey, here's some wishful thinking

He can hear me.

Hey, can't you?
This story
This is a ballad about me and you.

Oh boy, oh
You, listen here
Brown eyes, tan lines
Why did you make me fall in love with you
When you should've drawn the line?

Why did you do
What you did
You know where I'm getting at
Why didn't you just tell me to back off,
Take back my dreams, take 'em in my fingers
And

Squish..

I'd never have been here
If it wasn't for you in the first place
You said you'd be there
But where are you now,
Hey?

If only I could pass this nightmarish reality
As an unholy dream
A dense fog, clouding my judgement
Clouding reality.

Unfortunately I took your words to my heart
Sitting in the cabin when your eyes pierced mine
like a shard

I wonder why you held me tight
I remember very clearly
When you'd said to me

We'll
Be
Together
Till

Infinity.

Photograph of Srishti Bose by Farheen

11.

We met each other
At intersections

Stranded in our lives,
Broken.
You were at your worst,
But so was I.

I helped you heal a broken heart,
While I was nursing mine
At the same time.
Showed you ways
To not let yourself fall apart.

While I was all over
Picking up pieces of myself off the floor,
Pulled yourself straight up and out.

She was never your cup of gin,
That smile,
That was worth all that hurt and pain.

And then I was back,
Tending to strewn emotions
Because helping you made me think I was getting
better.

But I think,
That's where I failed.
Because all that happened was

I
Only
Broke

Furthermore.

Graphics by Husnul "Oon" Shaikh

12.

Your thoughts,
Were but a mystery,

A poem to my mind.

You turned me wild,
You drove me crazy.

And then you left me behind.

Forget what could have been,
You forgot what we were.

Our love,

Your name on my lips,
My name on yours?

Never.

Your words,
But a rare collectible.

Like a diary of endless songs to sing,
But sing them, when I do?
Torrential rains with them, they bring.

Who am I to say anything?
What rights do I have?

For you'd told me not to fall in love,
Yet I kept slicing my heart in half.

So, it was my mistake.
Overlooking the signs,

Jumping the fence gate.
Because instead of having written myself
Into a portion of your prose,
Like a damned damsel, something that I never
was,
I got thrown into your

Bed
Made
Of

Thorn Rose.

Photograph clicked by Srishti Bose

13.

I am invisible ink
A million different words on your body
Still etched onto your skin.

Engulfed by my love for you,
You were ingrained in me,
Making me lose my senses and sanity.

But
For you it was never more than a sin.

And I'm left with nothing but just invisible ink
On your body, on your skin.

And when she touches your body,
I am nowhere to be seen.
For I was nothing but a chapter

Written
All
Over
You
In

Invisible Ink.

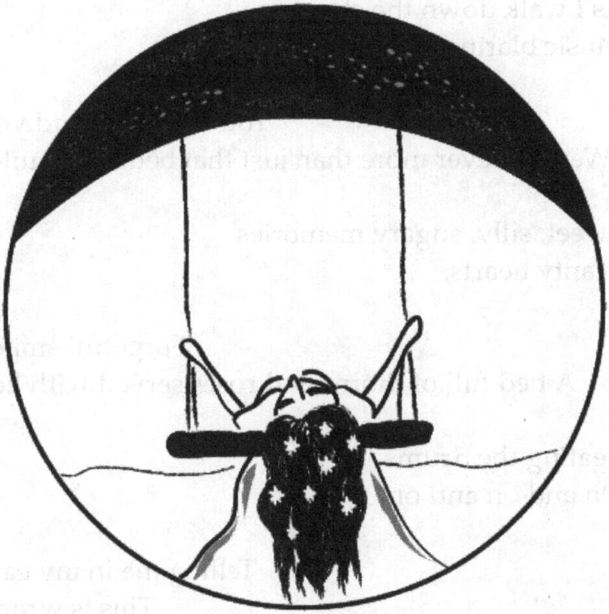

Graphics by Husnul "Oon" Shaikh

14.

As I walk down the street,
Music blaring loud, wondering

You and I, me and you,
Were we ever more than just that bedroom suite?

Sweet, silly, sugary memories
Scanty hearts,

Forgetful smiles,
A bed full of thorns and roses served with lies.

Beating the drums,
On and on and on.

Telling me in my ears
This is wrong,
Is wrong
Wrong.

But still,
I,

I looked into your eyes and saw love
Love like never before.

For you were my evermore,
My first.
Under the stars and the moon,
We laughed under that sky so blue.

You were all my colours,
My never changing hue.

But maybe,
Just maybe,
I was not
Maybe never at all,
In your skyline.

Never
At
All
In
Your

View.

Photograph of Srishti Bose by Anay

15.

I should let you go,
That's the only thing I've been told.

But my heart,
Oh this blood pumping,
And beating,
And surviving vessel,
Got beat
By you.
Couldn't survive
That piercing gaze,
That crooked smile
Wish I could've seen through.

I'm supposed to walk away.
Situation says so
But the heart and mind are stay put one way.

You told me not to
Wish you'd have held me and turned me around.
Never let me had my way
Beat me to pulp when I told you I'll stay.

But you're
Going
Going
Gone.

What? I understand the signs,
History repeats itself,
And so you, following the footsteps of everyone
You're leaving me too; it's called - to abandon.

While I'll still be there
Wondering

Our
Thing,

Us,

What was it?

Inconclusive.

Photograph of and by Ambuja Naik

16.

You were mine
I was yours.

And this was our
Soul crushing fire
Burning us,
Scorching us,

Crackling desire.

Cool blues
Against our hues.

Skin against skin.

Touching,

And breathing,

And loving,

And kissing.

Heaving,

And sighing,

And gasping.

So much missing

And

Then

Nothing.

Original artwork by Nida

17.

And while you were away,
Not bothered, aloof

I let someone else in
Guess they did their job for you.

Devil reincarnate
Bless you both,
Because now I am in pieces.
Broken,
Shattered,
Gone,
Beyond repair.

And where there used to be a garden
Full of peonies
Are just stones
And withered leaves.

And the wind will blow
Taking all the leaves with it.
Fly away to a newer land
Leaving yesterday behind
Blowing away to a new tomorrow.

Gather 'round and regenerate
In the form of a new shape.

A
New
Name

Resuscitate.

Photograph of Nida by Riza Suraiya Khan

18.

Tall and fair,
You were every girls dream.

Why then why, oh
Did you have to pick me?

Every time I sleep,
Your face is all that I see.

I don't want to,
No.
Move away,
Go.

Sweaty palms,
Messy hair,
Laced mucus
All over my face.
Eyes so beady
Can hardly see.

Who's that distraught girl in the mirror?
Wait,
Is that me?

...Is that?

Why then why, oh
There's a hole in my chest.

C A N' T B R E A T H E

Didn't care, did you?
That wasn't so indiscreet.

It was easy for you to leave

Leaving
Me
Incomplete

I'll always be (won't I?)

Obsolete.

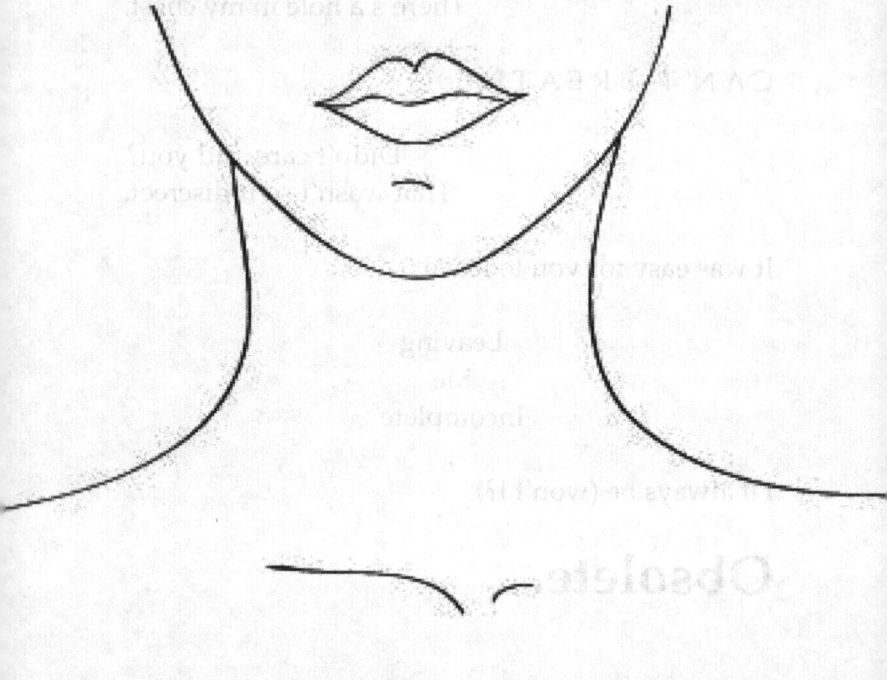

Graphics by Husnul "Oon" Shaikh

19.

Fade in,

Fade out.

Her sleepless nights,

A proof, no doubt.

Her nightmares,
He'd star in them daily.

On top of her,
Hovering,
Muffled,
Hurting,
Breaking.
Under him,
She,
Cowering.

Wake up,
Sweat.
And tears.
And pain.
And emptiness.

Hollow,
So hollow.

Morning,
Bedsheets,
And the mirror.
Who's that girl wearing her skin?

So bright, and sunny,
Yet so dark from within.

He strangled her shrieks,
Her helpless shouts,
And best of all?
It was daytime,
But if lights could cheat,

Fade
To
Black

Lights Out.

Graphics by Husnul "Oon" Shaikh

20.

'Pop in a pill',
They said
'It'll be better
Pop in a pill'.
I did
To free my mind of the clutter.

From the mess it is,
To the way it was.
Maybe I'll bleed to death (maybe I did)
Hey, could you pass the gauze?

Oh wait,
They say I've lost the plot,
Beat myself mental over you
But no,
I'm fine.
For when I look in the mirror,
All I am is
Rancid,
Cold and
Blue.

Blue
Blue blue blue
Blue blue

Not dying, not even screaming,
Just, the color of depression.

Too many pills maybe?
But hey,
Realization,
As light shines through
Beyond the horizon.

Blue, blue, blue, blue
My favourite color,

Blue,
Blue blue
Also, my

Favourite
Shade
Of

Poison.

Photograph of Nida by Riza Suraiya Khan

21.

They told me a girl lived down there,
The heart and soul of the place.
She was the life of this town,
They told me the girl lived there, she was.

Once upon a forgotten time,
That was her home.
The town, her house
And the people, hers.

But then came a strange being,
Took her away with him.
He took her so far and away,
Far behind even the reach of the skies.

She went and all was gone,
She went and the soul was lost.
The town no more smiled,
The town no more rejoiced.

Lost in the whirlwind,
She was taken.
Walking me down the road,
They narrated.

The story was sad,
It felt... real somehow.

The more they spoke of her,
Her story seemed just more than a story now.

A nerve was touched,
The breathing sharpened.
As we reached near the house,
They all took an expectant pause.

Stopping in their tracks,
They looked up at me,
As if waiting for something to happen,
Expecting something that I couldn't quite
understand.

Hopes diminished, they shook their heads,
Crestfallen, as if, they moved forward.
The doors opened,
And lo and behold.

I entered the house,
And it was as if something hit.
My eyes burned,
And throat went dry.

Unexpected tears streaming down my face,
I looked around.

It was... astonishing?
More so, confusing.

They told me they'd be introducing her to me,
This was quite the unexpected.
For the House of Mirrors it was,
Staring back, who else could be,

I realized the girl they said,

That
Girl
Was

Me.

Photograph of Nida by Riza Suraiya Khan

22.

So beat up,

Hurting,
Choking,
Dry eyes.

Tears that start at midnight.

Morning come
Morning go.

Smile plastered across the face.

As real as real gets,
Trust me it's original.

Never did I put on a show,

Can't.
Won't.
Never.
Not now.
Not ever.

Are you thinking the same?
Maybe.
Yeah,

Maybe
I
Ain't
Sane.

But, definitely.

Bipolar.

Graphics by Husnul “Oon” Shaikh

23.

With every wound I go in deep,
All my wounds on tether end.
Seems like someone's drowning me,
I can't breathe.
Help me I can't breathe.

Scaffoldings unfolding,
Voices overpowering.
I went so far but it's still pulling me near,
I can't breathe.
Help I can't breathe.

You fooled me once,
You fooled me twice.
Yet the corpse ain't you, but it's me,
I can't breathe.

Help. Can't. Breathe.

Pull me out but throw me down,
Pick me up, you swerve me around.
You disown me, but when did you own me?

I can't breathe.
Can't. Breathe.

Now I'm gone,
The memories torn.
Like a bedsheet stained,
Like veins deveined,
Like the first period blood,
Like a forceful thrust,
Like a knife's jab,
Like an unheard scab,
All stored in forever,
Like a filed register.

Souvenirs, unwanted,
Impressed forever upon us.

I
Can't
Breathe

I. Can't. B r e a t h e.

Photograph of Nida by Riza Suraiya Khan

24.

Tonight
Is one of those nights
I can smell you
And feel you.

My head pressing against your heart,
Listening to you breathe.
Sigh against sigh,
Your arms around me,
Making me feel loved
Making me feel safe.
I want you to be here.

Tonight
Is one of those nights,
I can smell you,

Lying under the stars,

Holding hands,
Everything seems right.

But you're not here,
We are not there.

That was a beautiful dream,
Something I'll be living on repeat.

I don't want to come back.
Why do we have to come back?

To
This
Unfair,
Bittersweet,

Reality.

Photograph of Srishti Bose by Ashutosh

25.

I think I just came into his life,
Only to make him realize,

How much more there was to this
How much more there was to live.
I gave him
My smiles,
My thoughts,
My laughter.

Brought him out of his
Self-induced stupor.

For all that I gave him,
My love.

All that I got back in return,
His lies.

But I still remained,
Standing always by his side.

Will he ever realize?
He easily walked in and out of it.
While I was right there,
Left,

Forgotten
Maybe (?)

Catatonic.

Photograph of Srishti Bose by Pooja Pandey

26.

For them
Her night was lit.

While she sat and gazed above.

For them
All was well.

But no one knew,
Her night had shifted hue.

The black and white was now painted,
To different shades of mauve and blue.

If only one could hear
What she wanted to say.

Her love,
Under construction.
Wedding night,
Hers.

But with his lover,
He ran away.

For them,
All must be well.
But her life,
In all honesty had.

An
Incredibly,
Unwanted,
Living

Hell.

Photograph of Nida by Nida

27.

I'm trying, okay?
I'm trying.

Trying to meet other boys,
Find who I need to find.
But, you know what?
I can't.

I can't and I won't.
Because they are,

And always will be,
The misfits.

Because their eyes
Aren't the shade of brown I can stare into,

Endlessly.

Because their hair,
Isn't the messed up hair
I love to keep fixing.

Because theirs aren't the shapely fingers,
I can slide mine through.

Because theirs aren't the lips,
That make me feel

As though I could breathe again.
Because
They
Aren't
You.

And because
You're the only one

With
Whom
I

Fit.

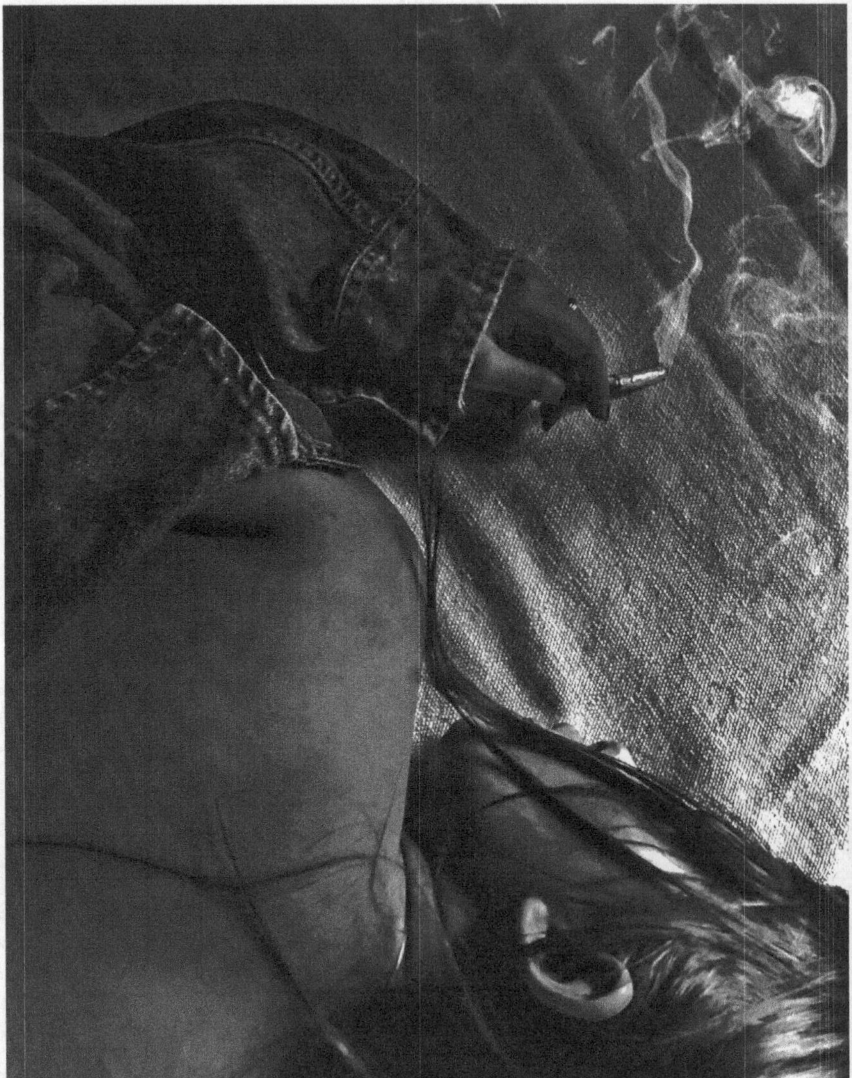

Photograph of Nida by Riza Suraiya Khan

28.

Hey you,
You.

You keep
Breaking my heart some more,
On repeat.

And then
Just like the seashells,

I'll keep picking my shattered self
Off of the shore.
For I love you,
And I'll always do.

One of those things,
Innit?
One of those many we share,
Betwixt.

Neither you,
Nor I can ever change this.

Sigh.
Another though,
Will always be in the run.

The one I always end up facing the brunt.
Guess this one thing,
Though,

Will remain a constant.
If nothing else does remain
You and I,
We,
These,

We
Can
Never
Change

Habits.

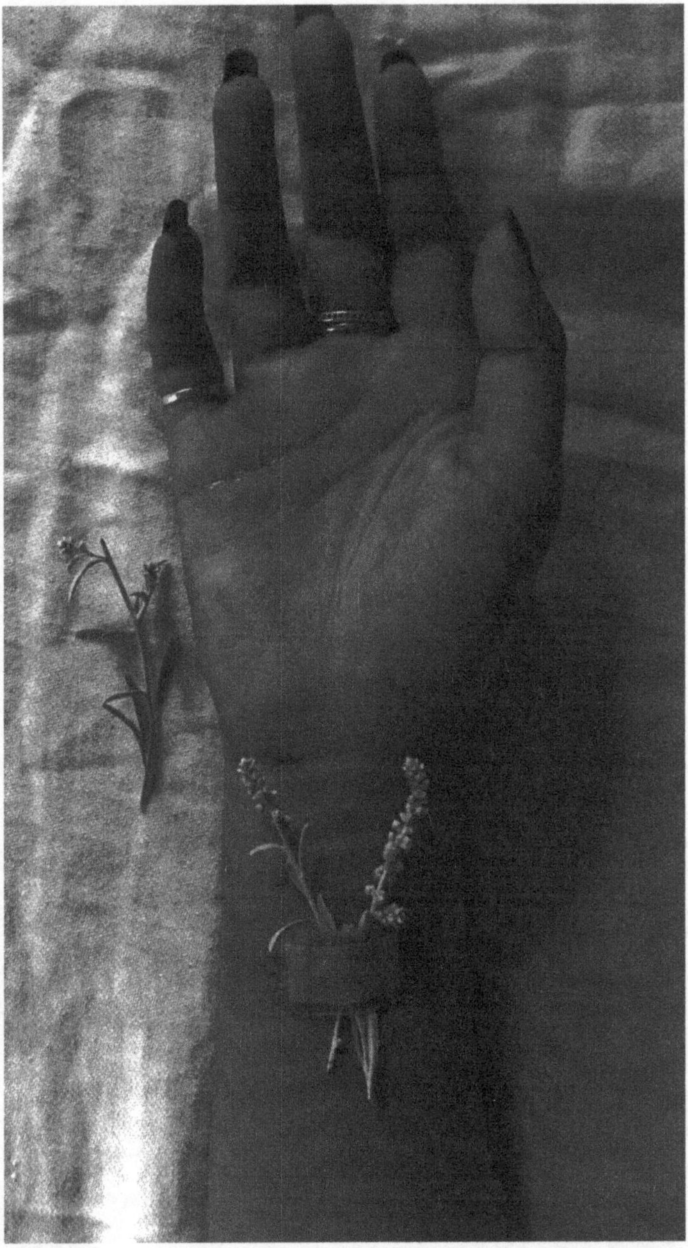

Photograph of Nida by Riza Suraiya Khan

29.

He said
Let's
Pretend
To not have met
To not have spent time together
To not have fallen in love
To not have broken apart.

Let's
Go back
In time
And get back to being two people,

Working under the same roof
Where I was the HOD,
Let's get our traces off of each other's memories.

But,
I quipped,
What do we do,
What do we do of what you've left with me.

I just said - he starts to say
No.
I cut him off,
I'm not talking about your bloody memories.

What am I to do with this damned baby,
The one that you put in me.

What do I do,
Hey

Tell
Me,
Hey.

Tell me?

Photograph of Srishti Bose by Ashutoṣh

30.

Maybe I'll never believe in love again,
But don't worry, it's not your fault, it's mine.

Maybe I'll never fall in love again,
But don't worry, it's not your fault, it's mine.

I prioritized you, even after all that's going around,
I prioritized you, even after you tried to burn us down,
I prioritized you.

Oh honey,
Why did I prioritize you.

You know I'd travel all the distances to meet you,
To minus the gap between us.
I am that crazy.
About you.
About us.

But this time you called me and said,
Asked me to meet you and gave your word,
You said you'll come, you promised.

I smiled, And I waited.
And I waited.

And I waited.

I'll call you back in a minute you said.
A minute?
A minute turned to ten,
Ten minutes to half an hour.
One and a half hour.
Two.
Three.

Smiles turned to tears,
And minutes turned to hours.
In the middle of nowhere and in the middle of the night,
You left me not just crying but scarred,
And,
Alone
And deserted.

Sitting at the pavement.
Waiting.
And waiting.
And waiting.

And then, just when I thought you would
Neither your call came,

Nor You.

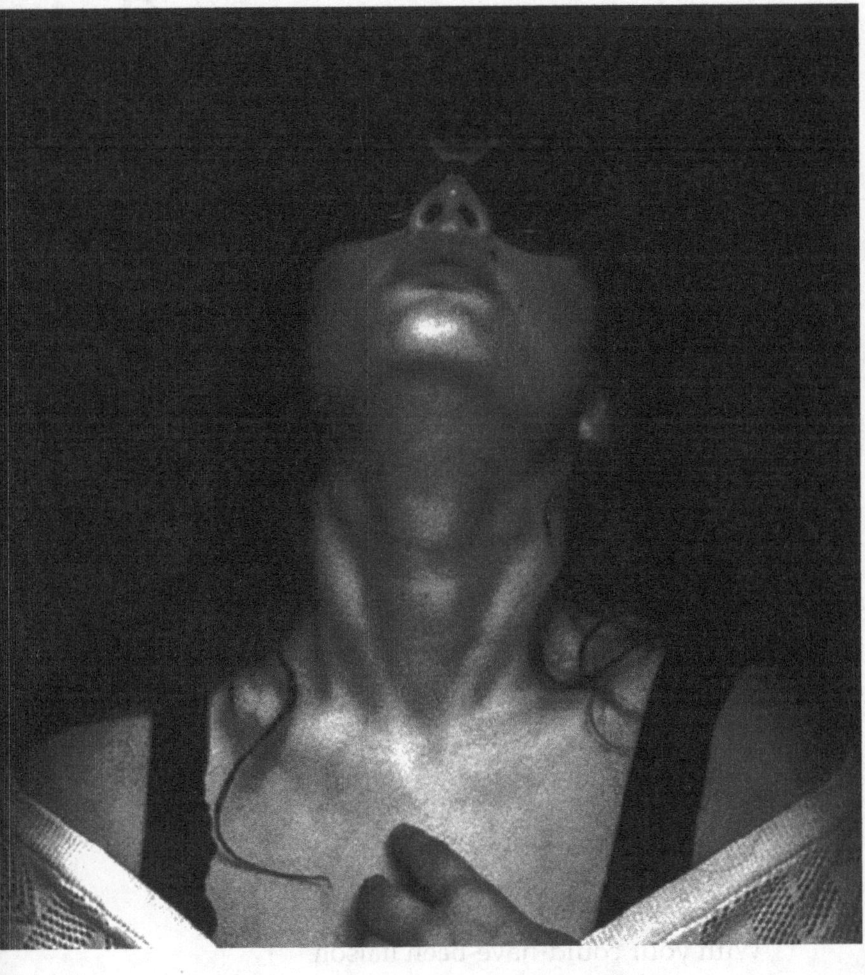

Photograph of Srishti Bose by Pooja Pandey

31.

You don't get to come back into her life,
And tell her,
That it's complicated.

What is complicated,
Is the girl you left behind.
With your baggage,
Added to her life.

Her own dramas to deal,
Them scars ,
That would never heal.
That story of hers,
Unheard.
Once free, she was now life's caged bird.

Victim to instances,
Experiences,
Unwanted changes.

She was the unmentionable mention.
You broke her,
With your could-have-been liaison.

She loved you,
But you didn't.

And somewhere,
In the story of her own life,

She
Became
The

Antagonist.

Photograph of Tejaswini Divya Naik by Ambuja Naik

32.

Weirdly enough,
She realized,
Deep into the chapters,
That they were just the pages of a book,
A cosmic wordplay.

Just a few words strewn together,
With a twist and a bend,
With she being his prologue,
And he being her end.
But, while they played the perfect characters,
Her emotions lagged
And in the end
She transpired to be his cliffhanger,
While he chose to be her

Climax.

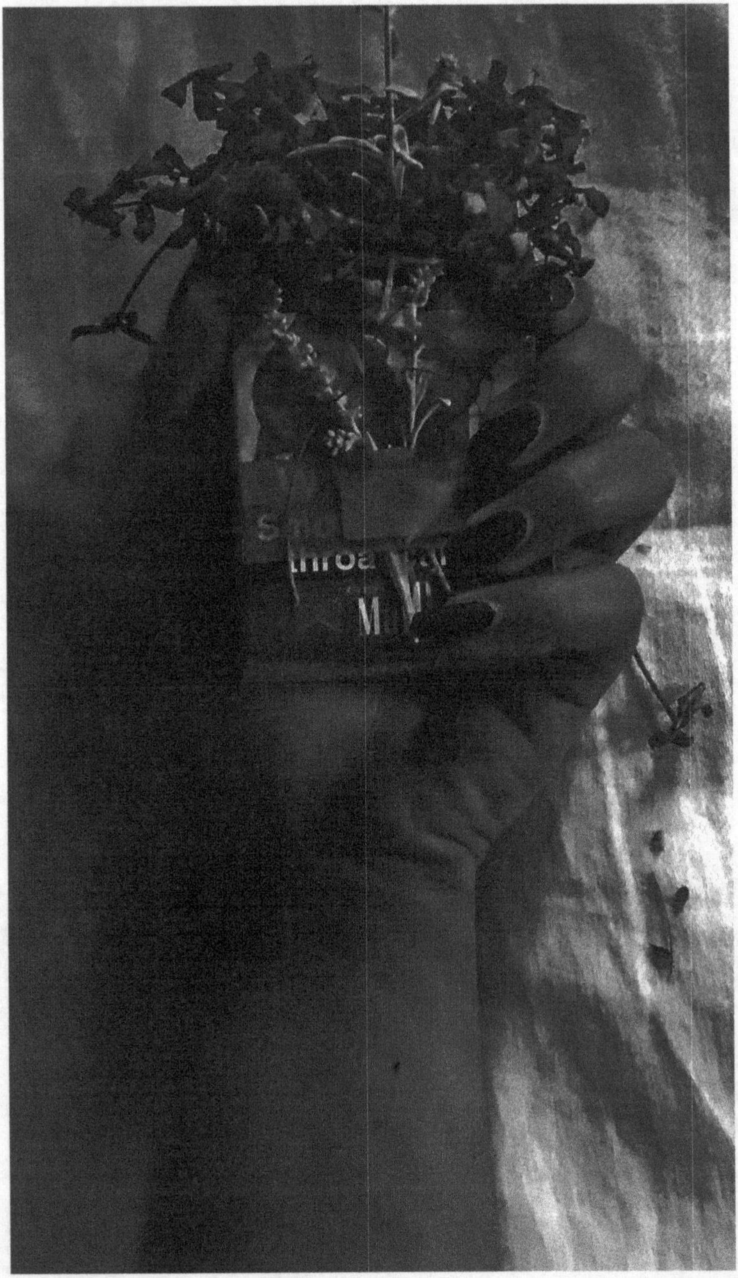

Photograph of Nida by Riza Suraiya Khan

33.

Breathing in sighs of despair,
A life beyond repair.
Threads broken, strands silken,
Strong at the front, but soft within.

Long, deep breaths,
Clenched fists.
Fighting back myself,
Choking, held back in.

I tell you, I felt it,
But, this couldn't really be.
Unresolved, yet frightening,
A closed book opens, reviving its tragedies.

The air had smelt foul,
Of Marijuana and Calvin Klein.
Every time he moved near,
Numb, my heart brimful of pain.

How do you get over it
When there was nothing to begin with.
How do you explain that to people?
That he took not just you,
But your soul and skin.

The more you rub, the more you peel.
The more the wound, singeing the heal.
A glowing dart, a flicker in the tree.
Didn't you hear of what you sow, so shall you reap?

The time is coming, the time is near,
Nothing of what it's beginning to be.
A prelude to the end, much anticipated,
A final closing call to this

Book of Tragedies.

Photograph of Srishti Bose by Tejaswini Divya Naik

34.

She was broken,
She was hurt.
But in you,
She found comfort.

You gave her feelings,
You gave her hope
She let down her walls,
She opened her doors.

She knew you through,
Your scars and your wounds
But you never asked off of her,
So she never told you.

In you she found
Reason.
She found solidarity.
She adored you,
Loved you.
She couldn't have been more happy.

And then the day of reckoning came,
She realized she'd been wrong.
All along.
For what she took as coming back home,
Was
An empty porch and a dark road beyond.

Let it happen to her again,
She did.
No one else was to blame,
But she
For he had always maintained
He was scarred,
But he would try,
Unsure if it would last.

Suffocated,
She felt,
Betrayed
By her own self.
Her head had said no,
But her heart had told her to go.

See what it's resulted in
She should have never let anyone in.

Her walls are going to be up again,
Stronger and unbreakable and fervent.
For she was okay,
But she was not.
And an oath
She took
To never

Let
Anything
Let
Her

Fall Apart.

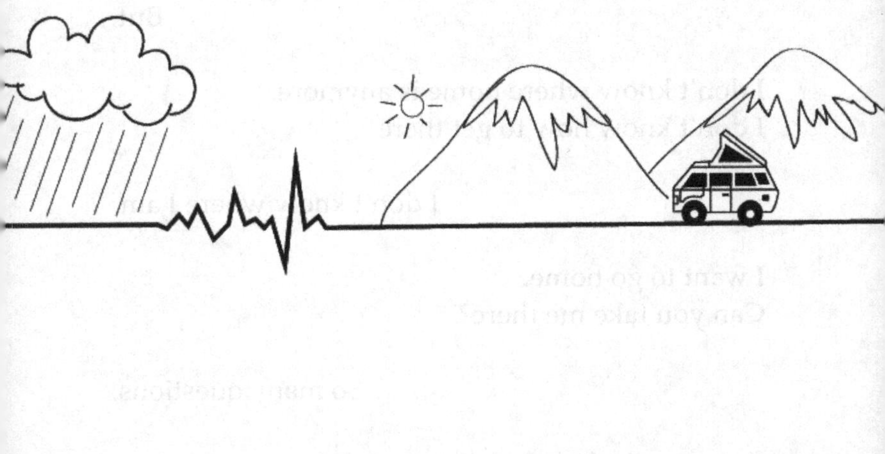

Graphics by Husnul "Oon" Shaikh

35.

Right now,
I'm just in a place that I don't belong.
And the only place I'd like to be is,
Home.

But,

I don't know where home is anymore.
I don't know how to get there.

I don't know where I am.

I want to go home.
Can you take me there?

So many questions,

But you won't answer me.
Why won't you answer?
I want to go home.
Take me there,

Please?

Photograph of Tejaswini Divya Naik

36.

My hair smells of smoke,
My breath smells of whiskey

No.

I am not fine
And probably,

Will never be.

Because, in the end,
I still smell of you.

And your smell is still ingrained,

Classic Milds and Issey Miyaki
Is any day better than my cheap

Smokes and Whiskey

PART 4 :
THE THEREAFTER

Graphics by Husnul "Oon" Shaikh

Photograph of Nida by Riza Suraiya Khan

37.

When
Pieces of me will be long gone,

When
Just you'll remain.

When people ask you who I was,

Then
Tell them, not, my name
Show them the skies.
Show them the butterflies.
Reminiscent to how we died,
Lifespan as long as a day.
So so funny, sigh.
Silly me,

I'd thought we'd survive
Silly me,
I'd thought we'd reprise
Silly me

Oh dear lord
Silly me
Silly silly me

Show them the grass,
Show them the whiskey.

The same one we'd laid on,
Counting stars as you'd kissed me.
I was a silly silly girl,
For I'd thought love was easy.
But who'd have known it'd blow apart my world,
Silly me,

Oh dear lord,
Silly me
Silly silly me.

Love wasn't easy,
You weren't any less.
Running, holding hands to the lift,
I looked at you and I thought I couldn't be more blessed,
For I had my man right beside me.

What was I to know,
You just took me to the top.
Only to throw me down when I was cradled deep in love, asleep.
Silly me.

Oh dear lord
Silly me
Silly silly me

So when people ask you,
Tell them the truth.
Tell them what you did to me
Knowingly.

That after all,
I wasn't silly all along.
It was just you,
And how I was just another

Victim

Photograph of Srishti Bose by Ashutosh

38.

You make me blue
Leave me bruised
Day after day after day after day.

You come back home
You shout and abuse
Day after day after day after day.

How am I supposed to live this way
Keep my mouth shut, hide my face.
Cover up the pain
Make it up away.
Hide it under blush and lipsticks
To only see you come back from office, your
cheek freshly stained?

You make me black
You beat me blue.
I won't ask where that lipstick stain came from
again,
Please don't lock me.
Please, the kids are watching.
I won't ask, I swear,

Please don't put me in chains.
But that's how you left me,
Only to OD.

You left little Sally to drown face first in the bathtub
As the neighbours heard my cry for help.
Called it in, but my baby was gone,
Little Sally was dead, it was too late.

And it is here I lay,
Under the stars and the moon.

With flowers in my hair,
Night after night after night after night.

Apologising to my little girl,
Couldn't save either her or myself.
But I've got to survive,
Night after night after night after night.

Blue.

Photograph of Nida by Riza Suraiya Khan

39.

Can I cry?
I swear I won't take your time,
I won't hold you or call you mine.
I'll only sit,
Won't utter a word.
For I know I won't be heard.

So,
Can I cry?

Over the drowning sun
Or the waning moon.
The fallen stars
Or the birds who flew
Past their bed time,
Over my head.
Clawed my eyes out,
Watered my bed.

Can I cry?
I know you don't like it,
You hate it to the core.
When I cry,
But does my weak
Make you feel?
I think not
Stone hearts don't heal.

So I will cry,
And let out my screams.
In the midst of the day,
In the deepest of your dreams,
I will haunt you.
For now and forever.
You will hear these wisps,
These sighs,
These sniffles,
I will cry.

I'll make you

Suffer.

Photograph of Nida by Riza Suraiya Khan

40.

I was dumb,
But I am not anymore.
I was a fool,
I didn't know what I had in store.

You had me all,
Through and through
Didn't think once,
When you're done, what'll I be without you.

Why did you do, what you did,
Why did you never realize, care or once see
Bleeding and broken and hurt is how you left me.

So far gone, is what I was,
Baby, oh baby, it is your loss.
Once bitten, twice shy,
Now try forever, ain't coming back, no no, not I.

I took you by your words,
Walked in straight, even though I knew I'd get hurt.
They warned me to not believe you,
But I was blinded by the love I had for you.

I was happy, I was free,
You made me be able to breathe.
Now see the irony, oh oh,
I feel I'm suffocating and I'm down under.

So far gone, is what I am,
Baby, oh baby, you didn't ever give a damn.
You broke me once, you broke me twice,
Now try forever, ain't coming back, no no, not I.

You always had her by your side,
I was just there as a standby.
If and if only I wish I knew,
I would have never let myself fall for you.

Now it is all done and the time is gone,
My tears have dried and I've moved on.
And you come to me, asking for an apology,
Forgive I will, but you want to come back to me.

So far gone, is what I am,
And now I don't give a damn.

Getting back together,
Don't build castles in the air.
When you should have,
You didn't bother, you didn't care.

Now how much ever you try,
Ain't coming back, no no, not I.
So far gone, yes I am

Buh-bye.

Photograph of Nida by Riza Suraiya Khan

41.

Dragging,
Heaving,
Heavy lifting,
This is not how it used to be.
Hurting,
Hitting,
Disgusting,
That's what this relationship is beginning to be.
Begging,
Pleading,
Hiding,
Now I'm in the cupboard, holding my knees.
One,
Two,
Three,
You're calling me out of my hiding.
Stifled,
Muffled,
A shuffle,
That's all it takes for you to pull me out,
And begins the scuffle.

Three,
Four,
Five,
I am yelling
You are screaming
I am gasping.Six,
You hit.
Seven,
You miss.
Eight,
I turn.
Nine,
You run.

Oh, dear lord, who's to blame?
Forgive me father for I have sinned.
It's the unbecoming,
Forgive me father.

For I killed my husband.

Game Over.

Photograph of Tejaswini Divya Naik by Pooja Pandey

42.

My hair still smells of smoke,
My breath, though, not tainted anymore
No more Whiskey through the day to take my breath away,
Reserved only for special occasions
And this day today, calls for an encore.

No,
I am not fine.
But
Soon
One day,

I know I will be.

Because now,
I smell like more of me,
Than I ever smelt of you,

Yes, it's true,
That your scent is still ingrained.
One of those things, ain't it?
That never goes, never will
Classic Milds and Issey Miyaki.
The essence of you, that I used to get high on,
But now its' over, I am gone.

I'm of Davidoffs and Marlboros.
And Issey Miyaki?
I got myself some of mine,
Yet still the best part is,
That nothing is, and nothing will ever be,
Better than my cheap

Smokes and Whiskey

;

I could choose to end
Everything
But I chose
To
Continue.

ABOUT THE AUTHOR

Tejaswini Divya Naik is an army brat, media grad, director's assistant and fierce activist. Her social media pages 'Satin and Gold' help her interact with thousands of young minds every day through poetry and stories.

Recently, Tejaswini's petitions on Change.org against YouTube and Zomato were lauded worldwide and won her a prestigious invitation to the Obama Foundation gala in Delhi to meet President Obama.

When not writing, you will find her snuggling with her Lhasa Apso named Muffin.

Other #SMBooks

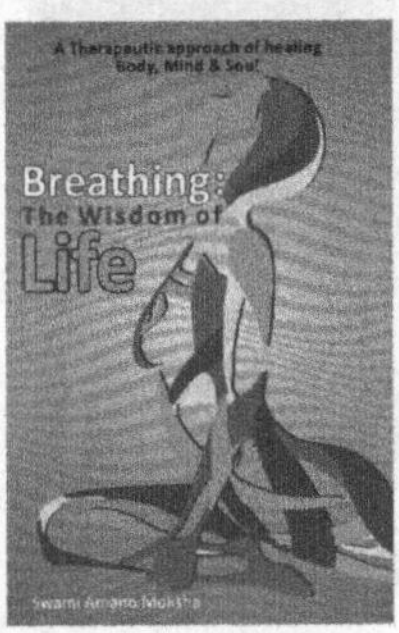

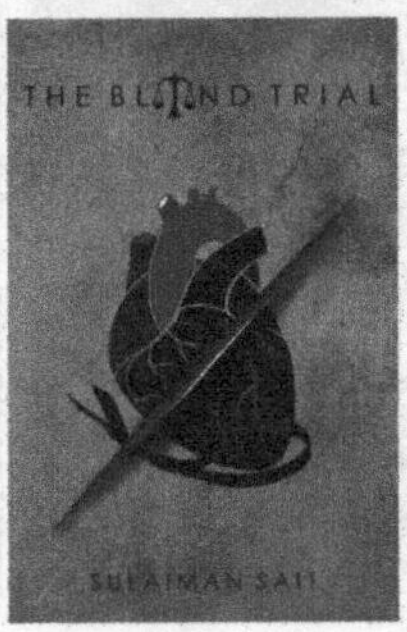

Other #SMBooks

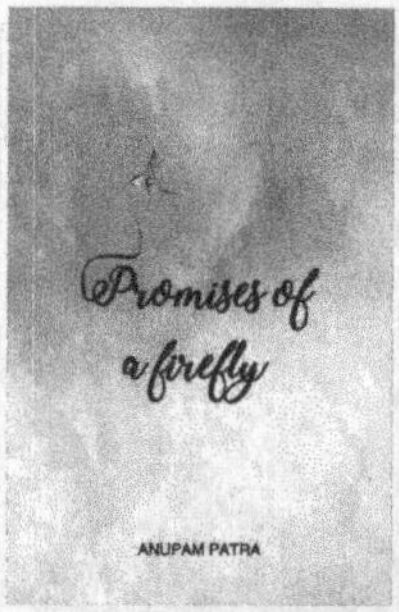